MAN IN A GREEN BERET

AND OTHER MEDAL OF HONOR WINNERS

by MEL CEBULASH

SBS SCHOLASTIC BOOK SERVICES
New York Toronto London Auckland Sydney

Photo credits: UPI, pages 17, 55, 64, 73; U.S. Army, pages 10, 19, 56, 80, 86, 91, 108, 113, 116; Navy department, page 43; Wide World, page 100.

Six stories in this book are based on original research and writing by Bernice M. and Stanley M. Ulanoff

2nd printing December 1969   Printed in the U. S. A.

Contents

Criteria for Award of the Medal of Honor   5

Introduction   6

It Was Either Military Service or Jail   11

The Old Sergeant   18

Ace of Aces   24

The Marine Who Wouldn't Quit   35

Day of Infamy — Fourteen Heros   41

In His Father's Footsteps   50

Poor Boy from Pittsburgh   57

Mosquito Squadron Commander   62

The Pirate of the Atlantic   72

Hero with a Personal Grudge   81

He Refused to Quit   85

Prisoner of War   90

Man in a Green Beret   101

They Called Him "Preacher"   107

Unarmed Hero   111

Eighth Cavalry Machine Gunner   117

Helicopter Rescue Pilot   122

Criteria for Award of the Medal of Honor

The Medal of Honor, established by Joint Resolution of Congress, 12 July 1862 (amended by Act of 9 July 1918 and Act of 25 July 1963) is awarded in the name of Congress to a person who, while a member of the Armed Forces, distinguishes himself conspicuously by gallantry and intrepidity at the risk of his life above and beyond the call of duty while engaged in an action against any enemy of the United States; while engaged in military operations involving conflict with an opposing foreign force; or while serving with friendly foreign forces engaged in an armed conflict against an opposing armed force in which the United States is not a belligerent party. The deed performed must have been one of personal bravery or self-sacrifice so conspicuous as to clearly distinguish the individual above his comrades and must have involved risk of life. Incontestable proof of the performance of service is exacted and each recommendation for award of this decoration is considered on the standard of extraordinary merit.

Introduction

Do you recognize the names of Sergeant Alvin York, First Lieutenant Edward V. Rickenbacker, and General Douglas MacArthur? Yes, these men were heroes who won America's highest military award — the Medal of Honor. But do you also recognize the names of First Sergeant Sydney Gumpertz, Gunner Jackson Charles Pharris, and Sergeant Cornelius H. Charlton? These men also won the Medal of Honor.

Why does one man gain lasting fame as a Medal of Honor winner, while another hero becomes forgotten almost overnight? Perhaps some winners capture the hearts and minds of the public. Or perhaps these same winners capture the hearts and minds of the men who write about Medal of Honor winners. More than likely a little of both is true, but the essential ingredient for lasting fame may be the war rather than the man. Heroes of the First or

Second World Wars are far better known to the American people than heroes of the Korean or Viet Nam Wars. Why? In general, the American people supported American action in the two World Wars without reservation. The same might not be said about the Korean and Viet Nam Wars, and the Medal winners in these wars disappear all too quickly into the pages of America's military history. This may prove especially true for the men who have risen "above and beyond the call of duty" in Viet Nam. It is a war that most Americans, regardless of their particular views, wish to forget, but as the toll of dead and wounded continues to mount, this "little war" in Southeast Asia becomes increasingly difficult to forget.

With Viet Nam's dead and wounded in mind, I have chosen to write briefly about Medal of Honor winners of wars during this century. Some have gained lasting fame, some are relatively unknown, and some have not yet been judged by time (the Viet Nam winners). Perhaps you'll be the first to learn about the latter group in the pages of a book. Or better yet, perhaps you'll be the last generation of Americans to read about war heroes with a first-hand knowledge of the terror, destruction, and death that accompany war.

Mel Cebulash

WORLD WAR I.

It Was Either Military Service or Jail

Alvin York was born in the mountain country near Pall Mall, Tennessee. His home was on the wild Wolf River, and there he learned the hunting, fighting, drinking ways of the rugged men who lived in the area. Then at the age of twenty-five, in 1914, a change came over Alvin. He joined the Church of Christ in the Christian Union and learned to accept as law all the teachings of the Bible, especially the Ten Commandments.

Over the next three years, Alvin's neighbors watched him change from a rough, tough young man to a quiet church leader. At the same time, his reputation as a deadly shot with a rifle grew, and he earned most of his living selling fox pelts. He received thirty-five dollars for each undamaged pelt, which meant that Alvin's shot had to go cleanly through the animal's head. Even for a sharpshooter, it wasn't an easy way to make a living.

While Alvin's reputation as a churchman and sharpshooter grew, his country's world problems also grew. In 1917, President Wilson announced that America was entering the First World War on the side of those countries fighting Germany. A short time later, Alvin received a postcard telling him that he was required to register for the draft. "I don't want to fight" was the message Alvin wrote on the card and then sent it back to the county draft board. War might mean killing other human beings and that would mean breaking one of the commandments. To Alvin, God's word on that matter was clear.

Alvin's draft board saw things differently, and it warned him that failure to register could mean a stiff prison sentence, so Alvin registered — as a conscientious objector because of his membership in the Church of Christ in the Christian Union.

The board ruled that Alvin's church membership wasn't reason enough for him to be excused from military service. Alvin appealed and lost. Finally, Alvin faced the decision of military service or jail. He decided to enter the army, hoping that he could serve his time in a peaceful way, but his hopes quickly died at Fort Gordon, Georgia.

Fort Gordon was the home of the 82nd Infantry Division, and Private York was assigned to Company G of the 328th Infantry Regiment. There his muscled body and excellent shooting caught the attention of Captain E.C.B. Danforth, the company commander. Captain Danforth soon learned that Alvin's conscience still troubled him. The entire division was training for eventual battle in France, and Alvin indicated that he would go and follow the commands of men, but he would hold those men responsible for making him turn away from one of God's commandments.

One night, Captain Danforth discussed York with the battalion commander, Major George E. Buxton. "It sounds as if York might make either a good soldier or a heap of trouble for you," the Major said. "Send him up to see me. I know a good share of the Bible, too."

The Major proved true to his word, and he cited several passages from the Bible to show Alvin that war, at times, was justified, but Alvin continued to stick to his beliefs. Finally, the Major said, "You're going home for two weeks before we ship over, York. During those two weeks, I want you to consider carefully this entire matter. When you get back, let me know what you have decided. If your conscience still bothers you, I'll try my best to get you released from the assignment. I can't promise that'll work, but I'll try."

Alvin seriously examined his beliefs during his two week leave, and just before returning to Fort Gordon, he decided that he could, in good conscience, fight in the war. It was a difficult decision, but once it was made Alvin never backed away from its requirements.

The news pleased Captain Danforth, and a short time later, he promoted the sharpshooter from Tennessee to private-first-class. Then the entire 82nd Division moved to camps in New York. There the soldiers made their final preparations for the trip to the battlefields of France.

In France, the division got its first taste of war in Lorraine during the summer of 1918. Alvin's fine shooting on the front lines earned him a promotion to corporal, and his reputation as a marksman soon spread from company to company.

Then on October 7, 1918, the 82nd joined with two other divisions in an effort to push the Germans out of the Argonne Forest. By morning, Alvin's platoon had moved well out in front of the division and crossed inside enemy lines.

The platoon soon came upon a large group of German soldiers, including a major. Not expecting Americans inside their lines, the Germans were caught off guard and quickly surrendered, but the calm was shattered seconds later, as German machine gun positions opened fire on the platoon and its prisoners. The men, Americans and Germans, raced in all directions, seeking trees and bushes that would provide cover.

When the heavy fire died down, only eight Americans were still alive. Of the eight, Corporal York held the highest rank, so he had to take charge. He and the others huddled against their remaining prisoners, hoping to get a clear picture of the enemy positions.

Alvin soon spotted the enemy machine guns, over twenty of them, within rifle distance to his right. "Start backing off with those prisoners," he told his men. "I'll cover you."

Alvin could see that the Germans would have to show themselves in order to fire their guns, so he wasted a few shots, planning to pick off the Germans when they popped up to locate the firing.

His plan worked. One German after another fell victim to Alvin's sharpshooting. Finally, a German officer led five of his men in a bayonet charge on Alvin's position. Whether they knew that Alvin had only a five-shot Enfield rifle, or that only one man held the position is difficult to say, but they did know that the other way they were falling like ducks in a shooting gallery.

Alvin knew that if he shot the lead man in the charge, the others would take cover and that would give them a chance to move slowly up to him, or, perhaps, surround him. So he shot the last man and then the next to last man. By using this old hunting trick, Alvin kept the lead men thinking that his shots were missing their targets.

After five shots, five Germans had fallen, but the last one, the officer, was too close for Alvin to reload his rifle. He quickly dropped his rifle and fired a shot from his Colt .45, killing the last of the charging Germans. For Alvin, who had hunted with a rifle most of his life, this pistol shot wasn't easy, but it seemed almost as if he couldn't miss that day.

The German major who had been taken prisoner earlier must have thought that Alvin couldn't miss, because he called to Alvin, telling him that he would get his men to surrender. Alvin let the major call over to the enemy machine gun positions, and soon the corporal from Tennessee and the men remaining in his platoon had 90 disarmed German soldiers marching toward the 82nd Division's rear position.

Once again, Alvin and his men found themselves cut off from the division by a force of enemy soldiers. This time, Alvin put a gun to the German major's head. The officer called for these soldiers also to throw down their arms, and they did.

When Corporal York and his men reached the safety of the American lines, their prisoners were counted and York was ordered to report to the brigade commander, General Lindsay.

Having reports of the Tennessee sharpshooter's amazing feats, General Lindsay said, "Well, York, I hear you've captured the whole German Army."

"No, sir," Alvin answered, "only a hundred and thirty-two of them."

Because of his brave exploits, Alvin was promoted to sergeant and was awarded the Distinguished Service Cross. Later, on the recommendation of General John Pershing, the commanding general of the American Expeditionary Force, Alvin received the Medal of Honor.

Perhaps Alvin York, up to now, is the most famous of all the winners of the Medal of Honor. In 1941, twenty-three years after his brave act and at the beginning of a new war, Hollywood made a movie of his life called *Sergeant York*, and a whole new generation learned of Alvin's heroic deeds. Then in 1954, men from the Bureau of Internal Revenue visited Alvin and informed him that he owed the government $25,000 in back income taxes. Old, sick, and broke, Alvin wondered what the government would do to him, but the American people had not forgotten Sergeant York. From every part of the country, they sent money — enough to pay Sergeant Alvin York's tax debt.

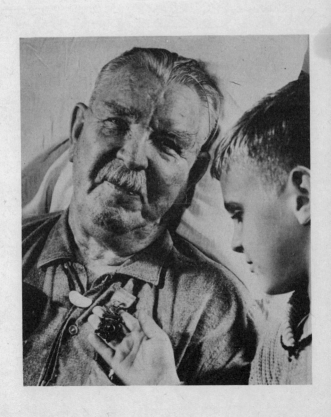

The Old Sergeant

Sydney Gumpertz was born in 1879 at Stockton, California. By the time he reached high school, he was six feet tall and quite muscular, so he joined the high school's cadet corps and worked his way up to the rank of sergeant. He liked the cadet corps, but even more he liked the idea of traveling around the country. So he quit school and left home.

Sydney traveled across the country, getting as far east as Washington, D.C. Then after several years of moving from city to city and job to job, he settled in Chicago and got married.

Sydney was thirty-seven years old when President Woodrow Wilson announced that the United States was entering World War I. Sydney immediately remembered his old cadet corps days and figured that he could help his country.

"You're too old," his friends told him. "The Army wants young men."

In a way, they were right. Sydney still had a muscular body, but the army wouldn't draft a man his age. Finally, Sydney made his decision.

"I'm enlisting," he told his wife. "If they don't take me, there's nothing I can do about it, but at least then I'll never have to be sorry that I didn't try."

The army took Sydney and sent him to Texas for training at Camp Logan. There he became a member of the 132nd Infantry Regiment of the 33rd Division and, in a short time, he gained the rank of sergeant. Sydney wasn't completely happy, though, because he was assigned to Headquarters Company. He wanted to be with the men who hit the front lines, not sitting the war out behind a desk.

A little later, there was an opening for a first sergeant with a company that would see action. "I'm the man for the job," Sydney told Company E's commanding officer.

"All right, Gumpertz," the officer said. "The men are rough on sergeants, but I think you'll be able to handle them."

First Sergeant Sydney Gumpertz was more than able to handle the men. He kept them so busy with their training that they had no time to give him trouble. Finally, all training ended, and the entire 33rd Division went to France in May 1918.

During that spring and summer, the men of the 33rd, including Gumpertz and Company E, saw some action and also many dead and unburied bodies from the battles of the winter that had passed. The men knew that the big battle — the battle for the Argonne Forest — would provide a chance to avenge these dead — or die.

Around the middle of September, Gumpertz and other men of the Jewish faith in the division got permission to go to a synagogue in a nearby town to observe their holy day of Yom Kippur. They were preparing to leave, when orders came down from division headquarters — make ready to move out. Gumpertz and the others rejoined their companies. They knew, as did all the soldiers in the division, that this was it — the push into the Argonne.

After nights of marching and days of hiding, Company E received orders to replace a French company, and on the night of September 25 Gumpertz and his men moved into the trenches and listened as their French allies disappeared into the darkness.

American and Allied artillery started firing on enemy positions a few hours after midnight. The plans called for the artillery to weaken the enemy and for Company E to move forward shortly after that and take the enemy positions.

So just before dawn, Gumpertz and the men of Company E moved out of their trenches and forward in the darkness. Lights from their own artillery exploding ahead of them made them a target for enemy snipers. By daybreak, many men had fallen.

The old sergeant and the remaining men in the fourth platoon had to cross a narrow stream, holding their rifles high above their heads. When they reached the other side, the men were soaked, and Gumpertz ordered that they rest and put on dry socks.

After a brief rest, they moved forward again, but an enemy machine gun pinned them down before they had gone any distance. A slight fog partially hid the gun from the Americans, but the same fog kept the enemy gunner from seeing the Americans. Knowing that someone was out there, the gunner swept the area repeatedly, lowering his fire every other sweep to get anyone who might have decided to crawl up on him.

Gumpertz called for volunteers, and two men crawled over to his side. "Here's what we're going to do," the old sergeant said. "When that machine gunner gets to the end of his sweep, we charge, following the sound of his gun. If we're fast enough and lucky enough, we can get to him before his sweep gets back to us."

Seconds later, the sergeant and the two volunteers raced toward the sound of the machine gun. They reached the gun faster than they had expected and almost fell into the hole in which it was set.

The machine gunner tried to swing his gun at Gumpertz and his men, but before he could, the sergeant fired his forty-five pistol three times, killing the gunner and the two men that loaded his gun. Then fourteen other Germans crawled out of the hole with their hands high above their heads.

Guards took the prisoners to the rear, and Gumpertz and his men continued on their offensive. Once again, they were quickly pinned down by enemy machine gun fire, and once again, the old sergeant got two volunteers to help him silence the gun.

This time, a German artillery shell burst on the

three advancing American soldiers, and Gumpertz's two volunteers were killed. Seeing that the men were beyond help, the sergeant looked forward and saw the machine gun about the distance of a pitching mound from home plate. At the same time, the machine gunner saw the lone American soldier and started to swing his gun toward him. Quickly, the sergeant pulled the pin from a grenade and threw the grenade, hoping that he would be in the strike zone. Then after the explosion, he charged.

"Come on!" he called back to the rest of his platoon. By the time the men caught up with the sergeant he had shot three more Germans. After taking over a dozen more prisoners and sending them back to the rear, the men moved out again.

Before Gumpertz and what remained of his platoon reached their final destination, the sergeant knocked out another machine gun nest with a grenade. This time, while his men provided him with cover fire, he crawled to the machine gun nest and gently slid the grenade into it.

For his bravery and leadership, First Sergeant Sydney Gumpertz was awarded the Medal of Honor. He proved that there are no special ages for heroes, only special times.

Ace of Aces

"Come on, Eddie!" With the wind whistling past his French Spad fighter plane, First Lieutenant Edward V. Rickenbacker remembered the screech of his tires as he used to round the turns at the Indianapolis "500" Speedway.

Suddenly Rickenbacker's attention turned to a flight of seven enemy airplanes! Rickenbacker quickly recognized five German Fokker D VIIs flying as protection for two Halberstadt observation planes. He knew that the Fokker D VII was the best single-seater fighter plane the enemy had. In fact, it was considered by many to be the best fighter plane of World War I.

Without hesitating for a moment, Rickenbacker dived his plane in for the attack. Disregarding the seven planes against him, he had confidence in his own ability and in the plane he flew. The Spad had a slight edge over the Fokker in level flight and it was faster in a climb. The Fokker, however, was more maneuverable, had greater speed and recovered more rapidly. It could also fly at a higher altitude and hold its position in a climb without going into a stall or tailspin. Both planes had two wings, were made of wood and fabric, and flew at little more than 100 miles per hour.

By this time, planes were whirling around in the sky in all directions. Rickenbacker and the Germans used every pilot's trick to maneuver the other into position for "the kill." Rick's fighter darted in and out among the enemy. He seemed to be everywhere. At last, he got his sights on a Fokker. Steadily he pressed the trigger. His twin machine guns came alive, spitting short bursts into the enemy fighter. The tracer bullets chewed a fiery chunk out of the Fokker's fuselage and down it went, out of control.

Once again Rick turned toward the enemy formation. This time he took on one of the Halberstadts, so he had to change his method of attack. A two-seater plane like the Halberstadt had a flexible machine gun mounted on a ring which the rear observer could pivot and swing from side to side. In addition, the pilot had his own machine gun in the front. Dodging the stream of bullets thrown at him, Rickenbacker closed in on the observation plane. He fixed the two-seater in his sights and again squeezed the trigger. Then the Halberstadt followed the Fokker, crashing to the earth below.

This was the battle near Billy, France, that won Eddie Rickenbacker the Medal of Honor for air action against the enemy. It took place on September 25, 1918. Rick's first combat flight had taken place a little more than five months before, but two of those months were spent in the hospital recovering from a serious ear operation.

On November 11, 1918, just a month and a half after his historic flight, the armistice was signed and World War I was over. Yet in his amazing short span of combat flying time, Rickenbacker became the "ace of aces." To become an "ace" a flier had to destroy five enemy aircraft. Rick destroyed twenty-six enemy planes, and this record made him an ace more than five times over. In addition to the Medal of Honor, he won some eighteen other decorations from the U.S. and its allies.

Rickenbacker was a racing driver when the U.S. entered the war in 1917, but he volunteered immediately for the Air Service. He also offered to recruit his fellow racing drivers for training as aviators. He felt that their training and experience would suit them perfectly for the job of fighter pilot. The new Air Service, however, would have none of it and his own application for enlistment was turned down as well, because he was twenty-seven years old and had a limited education. Nevertheless, Rick wanted to serve, so he gave up his $40,000-a-year income from racing driving and enlisted in the Army. Soon after, he was shipped to France. There he received a promotion to Sergeant and was assigned as driver for General John J. "Blackjack" Pershing.

Rick never gave up his desire to fly, and over and over again he asked for a transfer to the Air Service. It finally came through, and after he took

basic flight training, he was commissioned a
Second Lieutenant. Still he couldn't get into
combat flying, because the flying school kept him
on as an engineering officer. This was because of
his knowledge of engines and mechanics, and he
soon developed several safety devices and other
improvements. Once again his age was used as an
excuse when he asked for a combat assignment.
Once again, his repeated requests paid off; he was
assigned to the 94th Aero Squadron.

When Rick first arrived at the 94th in March
1918, the squadron was using French Nieuport 28
Scouts — a poor plane that often shed its wings
while in flight. Besides that, the squadron was completely unarmed. Major Raoul Lufbery, who was
assigned as an instructor to the squadron, was
furious. Lufbery couldn't take his pilots up against
the enemy without weapons. Finally, in early
April, the machine guns arrived.

Lufbery, now the Squadron's Commanding
Officer, took Rickenbacker and Lieutenant Douglas Campbell on the 94th's first combat flight over
enemy lines. Later, on April 25, 1918, Rick scored
his first victory.

He was flying alongside Captain James Norman
Hall. (Hall together with Captain Charles Nordoff,
also a U.S. flier, was later to write *Mutiny on the
Bounty*.) At this moment, though, Captain Hall
was engaged in a surprise attack on a German Pfalz
fighter plane. As Rickenbacker also dived for the
Pfalz, the enemy pilot spotted him. He twisted
away from Rick's attack, and Hall opened fire on
him from the other side. Taken by surprise, the

German tried to fly away from the attacking planes. Nevertheless, Rick stayed on his tail and moved to within 150 yards before he pressed his trigger. The bullets tore into the German's cockpit, and Rickenbacker's first victim hurtled down to crash on the ground below.

Less than two weeks later, Captain Hall was shot down and taken prisoner by the Germans. And in the next two week period, Major Lufbery was killed in a combat flight, so the 94th needed a new Commanding Officer. There were many officers with more rank and service time than First Lieutenant Rickenbacker, but the Chiefs of the U.S. Air Force decided that Rick was the man for the job. He was a born leader, an excellent mechanic, and a fine instructor. For once, his age was an advantage! He was also a skilled and precise pilot, so on the day he earned his Medal of Honor, Rick took command of the 94th Squadron.

Under Rickenbacker's leadership, the 94th scored more victories than any other American squadron. His pilots admired him, and the mechanics idolized him. Each group knew that they had a Commanding Officer who would never ask of them more than he himself could do.

By the end of the war, Rick, now a captain, had scored an amazing number of victories against the enemy. Yet his fellow combat pilots figured that he could have easily doubled his score, had he not had the responsibility of a squadron. Perhaps Rick sacrificed some personal glory, but at least he had the satisfaction of making the 94th the best squadron in the American Expeditionary Force — and a squadron to be remembered throughout the years.

It was Eddie Rickenbacker and his fellow pilots of the new U.S. Air Service that in little more than a half a year were able to fly against a more experienced, battle-hardened enemy flying force that had been at it for four years. But more than that, the Americans beat the Germans at their own game. What the Americans didn't have in experience they made up for by the use of better tactics, daring and sheer courage. In the end, U.S. airmen knocked a total of 927 Germans planes out of the sky. The Germans, during the same time, scored only 316 victories. The boys from big cities, farms, and ranches throughout the U.S. showed their German enemy that Americans learned quickly and well.

After the war, Eddie Rickenbacker returned to the Indianapolis Motor Speedway and became President and Director of that corporation. The war had given him a new interest, though, and a short time later, he climbed to top positions in the U.S. aviation and air transport industries.

In 1941, America once again went to war with Germany, and once again Rickenbacker showed that he still had the courage which brought him America's highest military honor almost a quarter of a century before then. He was sent as a civilian on a secret mission for the Army Air Force. The plane in which he was a passenger was forced to drop down somewhere in the Pacific ocean.

With only four oranges for food and without a drop of water, Rickenbacker and seven other survivors drifted helplessly in the ocean. They were lost for twenty-one days. Bobbing up and down, their inflated rubber life rafts. were constantly being tossed by waves of twelve-feet or more. Rick's leadership and courage kept them going despite their lack of food and water, the biting wind, the blazing sun, the cold nights, and the ocean which continually whipped into their open rafts. Because of a previous illness, one man died, but rescue finally came for Rick and the six others. Then they were brought to a hospital on one of the Pacific Islands. Rick was completely exhausted physically, but he regained his strength in a short time and completed his mission.

As a civilian, Eddie Rickenbacker also demonstrated the same leadership qualities, and he became the Chief Executive Officer of America's largest passenger-carrying air line — Eastern Air Lines.

WORLD WAR II

The Marine Who Wouldn't Quit

When John Basilone was a baby, his family moved from Buffalo, New York, to Raritan, New Jersey. There John grew up with his nine brothers and sisters. In 1934, John was strong, healthy, and eighteen, and like many other young men, he couldn't find work. Not wanting to spend his life on a street corner with other jobless young men waiting for the Depression to end, he enlisted in the U.S. Army for three years.

John liked the army and represented it in amateur boxing bouts during his first year. Then the army shipped him to Manila, and he soon found the Philippines and its people to his liking. There John finished his enlistment, and before he left he had "Manila 1936" tatooed on one of his forearms.

Back in Raritan, John found work. The pay was poor, but many young men still were out of work, so John considered himself lucky. He also turned to professional fighting for extra money, and although he wasn't a great fighter, he had the kind of courage that pleases fight fans.

Two years later, in 1939, World War II started. No one could say for certain that the United States would get into the war, but by the following year the government was drafting men just to be prepared. John didn't want to wait for his number to come up, so he went to a recruiting station and enlisted again. This time, he picked the marines.

The marines were considered by many to be the toughest men in uniform, so John figured that he was suited for the corps after three years of service and three years in the fight ring. In boot camp, John showed that he had figured correctly, easily getting through the most rigorous training sessions.

It wasn't long before John earned the rank of sergeant and was training young marines. The young men liked him and the stories he told about his old army days. From these stories and, perhaps, his tatoo, John was nicknamed "Manila" John.

Then the Japanese bombed Pearl Harbor, and shortly afterward, John learned that Manila had fallen to its Japanese invaders. He wondered what had happened to the girls that he had dated and the friends that he had made, and he dreamed of the day when Manila, his second home, would be free.

On September 18, 1942, the 7th Marines arrived on Guadalcanal as support for the other men in the 1st Division who already had suffered on the island at the hands of the stubborn Japanese foe. Leading a platoon in the 1st Battalion that day was Manila John.

In the weeks that followed, John and the others got as used to the bugs, flies, mosquitoes, and 100-degree heat as they could and waited for the Japanese attack that they knew would come. On October 24, the waiting ended. The Japanese Colonel Sandai Maruyama sent thousands of men forward. Their mission was to take the American's Henderson Air Field and crush every marine on Guadalcanal.

John's machine gun platoon heard the huge Japanese force coming through the darkness and heavy rain. Then the area below John's emplacement lit up, as the Japanese poured out of the jungle, firing and tossing grenades as they came in human waves. "Let them have it!" John called to his men.

Manila John's .30 caliber machine gun chattered away, and many Japanese fell only to be stepped over by the waves that followed them. John kept firing, hoping that his water-cooled gun would not overheat. Finally, it seemed as if the Japanese were pulling back.

Minutes later, they charged again, and again Manila John and his men held them off with heavy machine gun fire. After this attack, John raced off to get more ammunition. He returned in time for another Japanese charge.

All night long, he and the two men in the machine gun pit with him withstood the enemy charges. Each time a gun emptied or jammed, John rolled over to another gun, while the two men loaded or repaired the gun he had been using. Each time the ammunition got low, John quickly sneaked down the jungle trail and returned safely, though the trail was alive with Japanese soldiers. Several times, he and the other men had to fight off enemy soldiers who had reached the pit and leaped into it.

Manila John's leadership kept the pit going despite the overwhelming numbers of enemy troops who advanced against it. Then in the morning, Colonel Maruyama withdrew what remained of his once powerful force. The marines had stopped his thrust for Henderson Field.

The marines counted many dead Japanese soldiers on the slope that led into the jungle. Exactly how many enemy soldiers had been the victims of Manila John could not be determined, but thirty-eight of his victims were counted immediately in front of his gun emplacements.

For his action in defense of Henderson Field, Manila John Basilone received the Medal of Honor. About ten months later, John went home on leave, and the people of Raritan turned out for "Basilone Day." They cheered him and presented him with a five-thousand dollar War Bond.

Then John toured the country, selling War Bonds and listening to speakers who described his brave exploits to the cheering crowds. In July 1944, Manila John married Lena Riggi, a sergeant in the Woman's Marine Corps, in San Diego.

John had taken part in some of the most vicious action of the war. Now he could train other men for battle. "You did more than your share, sergeant," an officer told him. "There are plenty of younger men than you around. You train them, and they'll finish up the war for us."

John didn't see it that way. There still was a war going on, and the marines needed all the experienced fighting men they could find. Besides that, John wanted to be there when U.S. troops marched back into Manila. "What will my Filipino friends say if Manila John isn't there?" He asked one officer after another.

Finally, John got what he wanted. In September 1944, he went back to the Pacific with the 27th Regiment of the 5th Division.

Manila John stood on the deck of one of eight-hundred American ships poised for invasion on February 19, 1945. He watched, as the ships' huge guns softened up the tiny island for him and the others. It wasn't Manila, but Iwo Jima was a strong enemy position, and if it fell, the Japanese would know, if they didn't know already, that the end was near. He smiled to himself, thinking he'd get back to Manila yet.

Then the command echoed through John's ship, "Prepare to go ashore!"

With the calmness that comes with experience, John joined his machine gun platoon in the landing boat. "Load your weapons," he said. "When we hit that shore, you're going to get a good idea about how many Japanese are on that little island."

Manila John was right. When they hit the beach, the Japanese hit them with everything from artillery to rifle fire. An artillery shell dropped Manila John Basilone, and he died there on the beach at Iwo Jima.

As one of John's officers had once said, he had done more than his share. To some, perhaps, there was no reason for twenty-eight-year-old Manila John to draw his last breath on the beach at Iwo, but to John and men like him, their country's being at war was reason enough.

Day of Infamy – Fourteen Heroes

Only the prow of the once proud and mighty U.S. battleship *Arizona* remains above the waves. The rest of her shattered hull lies in the mud below Pearl Harbor, serving as a monument and final resting place for her gallant crew.

Every morning, to this day, an honor guard raises the American flag on the *Arizona* in the crew's memory — and in memory of other Americans who died that fateful day.

The Japanese launched a massive air attack against the unprepared and unsuspecting US naval base at Pearl Harbor on that bloody Hawaiian Sunday of December 7, 1941. Concentrating their assault on the row of battleships and the Army air base at Hickam Field, the Japanese planes quickly eliminated the United States power to strike back.

In a terrible few hours, the great *Arizona* was wrecked and lying at the bottom of the harbor. The battleships *Oklahoma* and *Utah* had flipped over and lay with their bottoms up. Also, the USS *West Virginia* and *California* were ripped, torn apart, and finally sank where they were moored.

Several other battleships, three cruisers, and three destroyers brought the total of damaged US Navy ships to nineteen. In addition, the Navy and Army Air Corps fighter planes that might have resisted the attacking Japanese were wiped out. Most of the planes were destroyed on the ground, before they even had a chance to engage the enemy. The runways were so badly bombed and cut-up that a take-off by surviving planes was impossible.

Despite all this, the real tragedy was the loss of life. Navy and Marine Corps dead and missing amounted to well over three thousand. This was more than four times as many as the total Navy losses in all of the sea battles of World War I and the Spanish-American War combined. And war had not even been declared yet!

For the surprised American forces, bravery and courage were the order of the day. The Navy awarded fourteen Medals of Honor for the magnificent deeds of daring and self-sacrifice performed at Pearl Harbor that infamous December morning. Ten were posthumously awarded to men who died while earning them.

Among these heroes was Lieutenant Commander Samuel G. Fuqua of the *Arizona*. Commander Fuqua rushed to the *Arizona's* quarterdeck when the attack began. Minutes later, the explosion of a large bomb knocked Commander Fuqua down and unconscious for a brief time. At the same time,

the large bomb penetrated several decks and started a severe fire.

Regaining consciousness, the Commander immediately took charge of the fire-fighting operation and the rescue of injured and wounded survivors of the explosion. Then another explosion forward made the ship appear to rise out of the water. Flames covered the whole forward part of the ship, and the wounded and burning were racing for the quarterdeck.

The bombs continued to fall and machine-gun bullets chipped away at the ship's deck, but despite these conditions, Commander Fuqua continued leading the fire fighters and rescue squads.

Finally, the Commander realized that the ship could not be saved. He looked for the officers who outranked him, but they were all dead. "Make way to abandon ship," he told one of the men. "Then see that the order is passed to all the men."

Still directing the rescue operation, Commander Fuqua remained on the *Arizona* until all its members that could be saved had been saved. Then when the last boat was loaded, he joined his men. Although many men were lost, Commander Fuqua's leadership and calmness under fire saved many men who also might have been lost.

The Medal of Honor was awarded posthumously to two other officers aboard the *Arizona*. Rear Admiral Isaac Campbell Kidd, Commander of Battleship Division One, of which the U.S.S. *Arizona* was the Flagship, and the battleship's commanding officer, Captain Franklin Van Valkenburgh. While discharging their duties, both officers died on the bridge when it received a direct bomb hit.

At the time of the attack, the U.S.S. *Vestal*, a repair ship, was anchored alongside the *Arizona*. When the *Arizona's* forward magazine exploded its blast lifted the repair ship's Commander Cassin Young from his deck and tossed him overboard.

Commander Young quickly swam back to his ship. It was afire in several places from bomb hits. Ordering his men to move the ship a distance from the *Arizona*, the Commander hoped to be able to repair his damaged ship and keep it seaworthy.

Despite severe bombing and machine gun fire all around him, Commander Young remained unrattled and determined that there was only one way to save his tilting ship. "Full speed ahead," he ordered. "We're putting her up on the beach." This courageous act saved the *Vestal* and many of its crew.

There was also Captain Mervyn Sharp Bennion, Commanding Officer of the U.S.S. *West Virginia*. Wounded mortally, Captain Bennion thought only about fighting and saving his ship. Because of his wound, he had to be carried from the bridge of his sinking ship, though he strongly protested this vain attempt to save him. Today, a destroyer in the fleet proudly bears his name.

Others were Seaman First-Class James Richard Ward and Ensign Francis C. Flaherty. Both men disregarded the order to abandon their ship, the *Oklahoma*, when it became apparent that the ship was about to go down. Instead, they each held flashlights in a turret so the rest of the turret crew could see and escape. In the end, Ward and Flaherty went down with their ship.

Chief Watertender Peter Tomich was another seaman who went down with his ship. He remained at his post in the U.S.S. *Utah's* engineering plant until all boilers were secured and all fireroom personnel had left their stations. By that time, Chief Tomich could not save himself.

Four of the *California's* crew rose "above and beyond the call of duty." They were Ensign Herbert C. Jones, Gunner Jackson Charles Pharris, Chief Radioman Thomas James Reeves, and Machinist's Mate First-Class Robert R. Scott.

Despite Japanese bomb and torpedo strikes, the *California's* antiaircraft gun crews stayed at their posts and managed to fire off some rounds at the enemy planes diving in around them. Nevertheless, the *California* suffered severe damage and soon the automatic ammunition hoists went out.

"Come on," Ensign Jones told a group of men. "We'll hoist the shells to the crews by hand."

His plan worked until another explosion wounded the Ensign and caused a fire around him and near the ammunition storage rooms. Two men rushed to the aid of the dying officer.

"Leave me alone," Ensign Jones told them. 'I haven't got a chance. You two get out of here before that ammo goes off."

Gunner Pharris, who had been promoted to Lieutenant at the time he received his Medal of Honor, was in charge of all equipment and supplies on the third deck when the first Japanese torpedo struck immediately below his station.

The concussion hurled Pharris up to the overhead. Landing back on the deck, the Gunner was stunned and severely injured, but he shook off the pain and dizziness and quickly set up a hand-supply ammunition train for the anti-aircraft guns.

Then a second torpedo hit tore up the deck and sent water, oil and oil fumes rushing in on the men. Seeing some of his remaining crew being overcome by the fumes, Pharris ordered the shipfitters to counterflood the damaged bulkhead.

Twice the fumes knocked out Pharris, but after each recovery, he desperately tried to speed up the flow of ammunition. He also risked his life several times, entering flooding compartments to drag unconscious sailors to safety.

His leadership and valiant efforts saved many lives and kept the *California* in action through most of the attack.

Elsewhere aboard the same battleship, Chief Radioman Reeves stood his ground in a burning passageway and continued to pass the ammunition for the antiaircraft guns. Finally, the smoke and fire overcame Reeves and eventually caused his death.

Machinist's Mate First-Class Scott stayed at his battle station in another quarter of the *California*. There he operated an air compressor and fed air to the men firing the guns in the turrets. As he and other members of the crew worked the compressor, their compartment started to flood from a torpedo strike. Scott waved the others out of the compartment, and he gave his life, remaining and working until the water covered him.

The battleship *Nevada* also had its heroes. One of these was Lieutenant Commander Donald Kirby Ross. Smoke, steam, and heat filled the *Nevada's* forward dynamo room and made it almost impossible for Commander Ross and crew to continue their duties. Worried about the lives of his men, Commander Ross finally ordered, "All of you men move out now!"

"What about you, Commander?" a seaman asked.

"Don't worry about me," the Commander replied. "I'm going to try to keep things going."

Alone Commander Ross performed all the duties, until the smoke and steam overcame him. Men sent to rescue the Commander found him unconscious on the floor of the forward dynamo room. They carried him away from the steam-filled room and managed to bring him back to consciousness. Commander Ross immediately returned to the forward dynamo room and after much work was able to get the smoke, steam, and heat under control.

Then he quickly moved to the after dynamo room. There the weary Commander continued to work until he passed out from exhaustion. Brought back to consciousness again, Commander Ross returned to his station, stopping only after orders to abandon his duties.

Chief Boatswain Edwin Joseph Hill gave his life while trying to free the *Nevada* so it could get underway and have a better chance of avoiding Japanese bombs and torpedoes. While enemy bombs and machine gun bullets poured down on

Pearl Harbor, Chief Hill and his line-handling men moved to the shore and cast off the *Nevada's* lines. Then he led his men in the swim back to the ship. Later, while attempting to let go the anchors, an explosion blew Chief Hill overboard, and several other bombs ended his life.

These, then, were the men who earned their nation's highest military award that bloody Sunday morning at Pearl Harbor. Fifty-four other heroes won the Navy Cross there.

December 7, 1941, marked the beginning of a dark period in America's history. Before the war would end, close to one million American servicemen would join the dead and wounded of Pearl Harbor.

In His Father's Footsteps

The naval task force had just halted their big gun's fire, and infantrymen were charging from the landing craft onto Red Beach. Fifty feet from shore, one of the landing barges crowding Leyte Gulf opened to release a party of officers. General of the Army Douglas MacArthur moved forward, paying no attention to the salt water drenching his sun tan uniform trousers to the knees. He had made good his promise to "return" to the Philippines.

To General MacArthur, the Philippine Islands were more than just a military objective. They were his home. Before the Japanese invasion, he had been Military Advisor to the Philippine government and lived in the Islands with his family for many years. But going back even further, his father, Major General Arthur MacArthur, a Medal of Honor winner, had been Commanding General of the United States Army of the Philippines. After that, he had been Military Governor and finally Governor General of the Islands following the Spanish-American War.

Perhaps as Douglas MacArthur waded through the Pacific waters that historic day, he was thinking of his father, but undoubtedly his main thoughts were for the brave people of the Islands — his lifelong friends.

At the outbreak of the Spanish-American War, Arthur MacArthur was named a Brigadier General of Volunteers and ordered to the Philippines. Douglas had already been appointed to the United States Military Academy at West Point, but instead he wanted to enlist in the Army and go to the Islands with his dad.

"Doug," Arthur MacArthur told him, "there will be plenty of fighting in the coming years, and it'll go far beyond this. Prepare yourself now!"

Douglas listened to the words that would prove to be true in less than twenty years and went off to West Point. Reflecting on that decision many years later, he explained, "My father was my idol. I emulated him not only as an ideal soldier but as a great man."

Then, as now, studies at West Point were not easy, but fortunately all was not work and study at the Academy. Cadet MacArthur played on the baseball team and was manager of the football team. And in 1901, he scored the winning run in the first baseball game played against the Naval Academy.

By the end of his four years at the Academy, young Douglas had earned the highest grades recorded there in twenty-five years, and the spirit of West Point had become his very life.

Douglas MacArthur's sense of duty served him well, and by the time the U.S. entered World War One in 1917, he had already reached the rank of Major. He was promoted to full Colonel then and assigned to the 42nd Division. MacArthur served with the division in France as its Chief of Staff, a Brigade Commander, and finally as Commanding General. Often he was cited for bravery and General Pershing, Commander of the American Expeditionary Force in France, said of him, "MacArthur is the greatest leader of troops we have."

Following the war, Douglas MacArthur returned to the Academy as its Superintendent, in command of West Point. Here he had an opportunity to help the school that had done so much for him. In the rush to get enough trained men to lead the rapidly expanding army that the U.S. put into the field in the First World War, the West Point course had been shortened to one year. MacArthur brought it back to four years and helped to modernize the curriculum.

Later, like his father, he commanded the Philippine Army, and when World War II started, he was in the Islands. President Franklin D. Roosevelt named MacArthur Supreme Commander in the Pacific Theater of Operations. The Islands had been overrun by Japanese forces, and President Roosevelt ordered his new Supreme Commander to break through enemy lines and get to Australia. There he could organize his forces to fight back against the Japanese.

Before Douglas MacArthur left the Islands, he again followed in his father's footsteps, winning the Medal of Honor for his courageous leadership in the defense of Bataan. This is the only case in American history where a father and son have both won their nation's highest military honor.

Forced to leave the Islands, the place he had come to know as home, MacArthur told his friends who were staying behind, "I shall return." Then he and his family left for Australia, travelling first by night in a PT boat and later in a bomber.

In 1944, he earned a five-star rank with the title of General of the Army, along with Generals Eisenhower, Marshall, and Arnold.

Later, Douglas MacArthur, like his father, became a Military Governor. Following the dropping of the atomic bombs on Hiroshima and Nagasaki, and the surrender of Japan, he became Military Governor of occupied Japan.

The call to arms came again for General MacArthur with the outbreak of the Korean War. United Nations forces, under his command, pushed back the North Koreans who had driven across their southern boundary — the 38th Parallel — into South Korea. General MacArthur also engineered a brilliant landing at Inchon that cut off the enemy.

Unfortunately, a complete victory wasn't to be gained so easily. As the Communist North Koreans were beaten back to their northernmost borders, whole divisions of Red Chinese "volunteers" attacked the United Nations troops. MIG 15 jet fighter planes flew from their bases in China to engage U.S. F-86 *Sabrejets*. Chinese troops and planes hit and ran to safety north of the Yalu River which our troops and planes were not allowed to cross.

MacArthur wanted to attack and bomb the Red Chinese, on their own ground, across the Yalu. This, however, was against United States policy. Our government did not want to become involved in an all-out war with Red China. Finally, President Truman exercised his right as Commander-in-Chief of United States Armed Forces and relieved General MacArthur of his command.

Out of uniform for one of the very few times in his long life, MacArthur advised another retired general, President-elect Eisenhower, on the Korean War. He lived in New York City at the Waldorf-Astoria Hotel, and there, in addition to being elected Chairman of the Board of Directors of the Remington-Rand Corporation, he wrote his memoirs.

MacArthur's last visit to his beloved West Point came in 1962. With sadness in his heart, he told the cadets, "Today marks my final roll call with you. But I want you to know that when I cross the river my last conscious thoughts will be of the Corps — and the Corps — and the Corps. I bid you farewell."

General of the Army Douglas MacArthur, after a long life of honorable and extraordinary service to his country, died in 1964.

Poor Boy from Pittsburgh

In 1941, boxing fans were shocked when Pittsburgh's Billy Conn came within minutes of winning the heavyweight championship from the seemingly unbeatable Joe Louis. That same year, all Americans were shocked when the Japanese attacked Pearl Harbor and forced the United States into World War II. Like Billy Conn, Pittsburgh's Charles "Chuck" Kelly had learned much about fighting on the city's streets, but the war became his first experience in getting paid for fighting.

Chuck Kelly grew up on the north side of Pittsburgh. His family was large and poor, and he and his brothers had their share of winning and losing battles with other boys in the neighborhood.

When Chuck finished grammar school, he announced that he had had enough school. The country was in the midst of a depression, and things were bad at home, so he could help by working.

He quickly found that work was scarce. He took odd jobs in the neighborhood, but most of his time was spent standing on street corners with a gang of boys and getting chased by the police who soon knew him by name. Above all, Chuck wanted to be a truck driver, but the teamsters were having trouble finding work for their own men. When Chuck could, he'd borrow a car and race through the neighborhood, dreaming of the day that he'd have his own truck or car.

Just before Pearl Harbor, he worked washing walls for a paperhanger. Then on Sunday, December 7, 1941, he heard the news of the Japanese attack. In the days that followed two of his brothers enlisted, and other young men disappeared from the street corners, so Chuck, too, enlisted.

Chuck volunteered for the infantry, hoping to get to the action as soon as possible. Although he gained somewhat of a reputation of being a sloppy soldier, he got through his basic training easily enough and then volunteered for paratrooper training at Fort Benning, Georgia. To him, the paratroopers seemed to be the toughest men in the army, and he figured that he should be with them.

As time went on, more and more men in training with Chuck ended up in the hospital with broken legs, backs, and arms. Most of them would get reassigned to outfits that would operate far behind the front lines. This worried Chuck. He had enlisted for action, and he wasn't going to miss that because of a practice jump from an airplane.

Feeling that he had made a terrible mistake, he went home to Pittsburgh to think it over. He was

absent without leave, but he kept that secret from
his parents until one of the local police guessed it
and threatened to tell his parents. Seven of Chuck's
brothers were now in the service, and he didn't
want any of them or his parents to think he was
running away from the army, so he returned to Fort
Benning to face a military court for being AWOL.

He pleaded guilty at his court martial hearing
and was fined twenty-eight dollars and not allowed
to leave the post for twenty-eight days. Also, his
commanding officer told him, "You're out of the
paratroopers, Kelly."

He soon received assignment to Company L,
143rd Infantry, of the 36th Infantry Division, an
outfit that drew most of its men from Texas. He
reported to Camp Edwards, Massachusetts, where
the division was making its final preparations
before sailing for North Africa.

The division was in North Africa long enough to
get ready for its real mission — a landing at Sal-
erno Beach in Italy. On September 9, 1943, Chuck
and the other men of Company L boarded their
landing boats and headed for the Italian shore.

As they moved closer to land, German artillery
shells and planes blasted the waters and boats all
around Chuck. Leaving the boat, Chuck pushed his
way through the shallow waters and onto the shore.
It was a madhouse of activity, and Chuck noticed
hundreds of dead and wounded soldiers spread all
over the beach. "Move inland!" an officer called
frantically.

Chuck followed the order — perhaps, too well.
He was some distance inland before he realized

that the other men from his outfit had gone in a different direction. He quickly doubled back for the beach, but before he reached it, he ran into two light German tanks. Hiding off to the side of the road, he fired on the tanks with his automatic rifle. Fortunately for him, they had no time for a lone rifleman and kept on going. By morning, he was back with what was left of his company, as it started for Hill 315 which overlooked the town of Altavilla.

Two days later, September 13, Company L started its push into Altavilla. At the outskirts of the town, heavy enemy fire brought Chuck and the rest of the men to a halt. They were pinned down by a machine gun, so Chuck crawled over to his company commander and asked, "Let me take a few men with me to see if we can pinpoint that gun?"

For a moment, the CO hesitated. Then he said, "Go ahead, but be careful. I can't afford to lose you or anyone else, Kelly."

Chuck and four other men located the gun in a few minutes, but they were driven off by enemy mortar fire. Then the CO sent word that Chuck and the others should watch the Germans, so the five soldiers worked their way closer to the machine gun.

Then a force of about seventy German soldiers spotted the Americans and rushed them from two sides. Chuck quickly fired a burst of rounds, silencing the machine gun and the three men manning it.

Suddenly the Germans charged Chuck and the others. Chuck fired a full magazine of rounds, reloaded, and fired another full magazine. When Chuck finally stopped, about half of the German force was dead, and the rest of them were falling back. Quickly, Chuck and the others moved back to the company.

Later that day, Chuck was sent back to Altavilla for more ammunition. Working his way through a heavy enemy attack, he reached the ammunition storehouse, but the officer in charge told Chuck that he would stay to help defend the position.

Posted by a window, Chuck watched the alley at the rear of the house the whole night, and when daylight came, German SS troops rushed across the alley, firing at the men in the windows. Chuck fired back as fast as he could, burning out four automatic rifles and littering the alley with bodies of SS men.

Nevertheless, the enemy had Chuck and the others outnumbered by so much that their chance of continuing to defend the position seemed hopeless. Then Chuck grabbed a mortar shell, pulled out the safety pin, and tapped the shell on the floor to loosen the secondary pin. Finally, he removed that pin with his teeth and tossed the shell at the Germans moving across the alley.

The house vibrated from the tremendous explosion. When the smoke cleared, Chuck could see several more dead Germans in the alley. He continued to throw mortar shells out of the window, until the word came that he and the others were to withdraw as soon as darkness hit. They left in groups of six, and Chuck was one of the last men out of the building, firing a final burst from a newly acquired automatic rifle.

For his heroism on September 13, 1943, Corporal Charles "Chuck" Kelly was awarded the Medal of Honor, and in 1944, the people of Pittsburgh lined the streets for a parade honoring the poor boy from the north side. Chuck, by then a sergeant, had earned a new nickname — "Commando" Kelly.

Later, his medal brought him money, as well as fame. He sold his life story to a magazine and also to a Hollywood producer. The movie was never made, but his story was read by people all over the country.

Mosquito Squadron Commander

"Steady as she goes!" the command rang out crisp and clear in the Pacific air.

"Steady, sir," said the quartermaster at the wheel, over the roar of the three Packard engines. Their 4,200 horse power pushed the trim craft through the water at speeds up to 84 miles per hour. Then as the little boat knifed through the waves of Manila Bay, the rugged Naval Officer on its bridge stared at the bombers in the sky overhead.

The date was December 10, 1941, three days after the surprise Japanese attack on Pearl Harbor. Warned that the Japanese now planned to bomb Manila, the Navy ordered Lieutenant Commander John D. Bulkeley to take his Motor Torpedo Boat Squadron Three into the bay, hoping that the order would be safe away from the shore.

The small ships cruised in the bay's waters, and

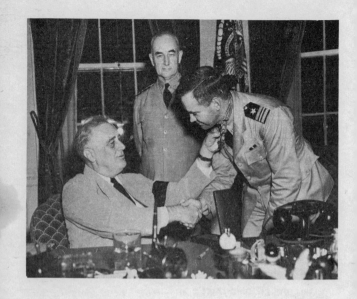

their crews watched as enemy bombers dropped bomb-load after bomb-load on the city of Manila. After that, the enemy bombers wiped out the large U.S. Naval Base at Cavite and attacked the shipping in the harbor. "Where are our planes?" several men on the small ships called out.

Sometime later, the crews learned that only three Army Air Corps fighter planes were left in the Philippines. The others had been wiped out — on the ground. And the PT crews also learned how useless the antiaircraft guns had been. They had a range of 10,000 feet, but the enemy bombers hit at their targets from a safe 15,000 to 20,000 feet.

Suddenly, as the PT crews watched the destruction, five enemy dive bombers peeled off their formation and swooped down, heading for the small boats. "Scatter!" Commander Bulkeley ordered.

There was no time to relay the message, so the Commander's quartermaster spun his wheel and weaved in and out of the bombs dropping around them. The rest of the squadron followed its lead boat and twisted and turned to make as poor a target as they could. At the same time, the PT's machine guns chattered away at the attackers. The bombers were zooming in low, and the sailors could clearly see the Japanese flags on their wing-tips.

Each boat had two sets of double mounted .50 calibre machine guns, one set on the port side, the other on the starboard. Teaming up, the gunners on each boat picked a target and blazed away at it. This was their first action against the enemy, and after seeing the destruction of Manila, the gunners were eager to draw blood. They aimed and fired with a calm, cool vengeance! Soon enough their teamwork paid off. PT 31 knocked one bomber out of action and watched it, trailing smoke, crash into the bay. Then the gunners of PT 35 felled an enemy bomber. Despite the losses, the bombers kept up their attack until two more of them were dropped into the bay by the marksmen of PT 31. The remaining bomber roared off. The mosquito's sting had been felt. Not one of the little PTs was even scratched.

Seeing that the other enemy bombers were headed for home, Bulkeley signaled for his squadron to return to Cavite. Once there, the Navy men saw, at close hand, the awful death and destruction that had poured down from the sky. What had been a powerful naval base was now a flaming mass of twisted steel and wreckage. Motor Torpedo Boat Squadron Three's spare parts, motors, torpedoes, and fuel had also gone up in the flames.

Nevertheless, there was no time to worry about fuel or parts. Men were dying. The little boats were turned immediately into "floating ambulances" to carry the wounded across the bay to the Army hospital at Corregidor. Over and over again, the boats made the short trip. It was a grim task, and by the time it ended, the sailors were slipping in the blood covering their decks.

This was one of many duties for the PTs of Motor Torpedo Boat Squadron Three. They served as messengers, carrying papers from one end of the islands to the other when communications were cut. They patrolled the waters and carried supplies.

And they also did their most important duty —
sinking enemy ships.

The PTs were amazing little boats. They were
made of plywood and measured 70 feet in length
and 20 feet in width. The boats had no armor, but
their speed, maneuverability and four torpedoes
(two on each side) made them a good match for the
mightiest of the Japanese cruisers and battlewag-
ons. They were the Davids against the Goliaths of
the enemy navy. Six of these fighting boats, PTs 31,
32, 33, 34, 35, and 41 made up Lieutenant Bulkeley's squadron. They, together with the lieutenant's
hand-picked crews (twelve to a boat), had arrived
in the Philippines in the fall of '41. Their commander had prepared them for any possible event,
so on December 7th they were ready.

John Bulkeley, from New York City, was 30
years old at this time. Eight years before he had
been graduated from the Naval Academy at
Annapolis. After that, he had married and later
became the father of a girl. He was a good sailor
and an excellent commander.

Bulkeley felt that his little PTs were ready for
any enemy warships, and he waited for orders to
strike. He didn't have to wait long. Word came
down that the Japanese had already invaded the
Philippine Islands, and one of their cruisers was
shelling the trapped American troops and their
artillery positions on Bataan. An Army officer had
requested relief, so the Admiral sent orders for
Bulkeley.

The Commander selected two of his boats —
numbers 31 and 34 — and waited for darkness. At

2100 hours (9 P.M.) they left, Bulkeley in PT 34 and Lieutenant Edward G. De Long commanding PT 31. The sea was rough, so Bulkeley cut the boats' speed to 35 knots per hour. Then he glanced at the instruments in front of him. They were heading for Subic Bay on the west coast of the Island of Luzon. Inside Subic was a smaller bay called Port Binanga. That was where the Japanese cruiser was hiding. It had the added protection of its own shore gun batteries close at hand.

Bulkeley's plan was for the two small boats to enter Subic Bay at the same time, one boat making a sweep of the right side of the bay and the other the left, meeting at Port Binanga. If there was a delay, or something went wrong, they were to meet at daybreak outside the mine fields of Corregidor. They arrived at Subic Bay shortly after midnight. As planned, Lieutenant De Long took his boat to the right, and Bulkeley started his sweep over the left side of the bay.

"Full speed ahead!" the Commander ordered, making use of the calm waters of the bay.

"Aye, sir," a man tending the engine answered. Seconds later, the boat lunged forward and skimmed over the water.

The bay, which had been black and still, came alive with the roar of the PTs' motors. Fingers of light pushed through the darkness, feeling for the speedy little boats. The crews could hear the screech of the artillery shells all around them and feel the geysers of water from their bursts. Half an hour later, Bulkeley and his PT 34 were at the entrance to Port Binanga.

For a moment, Bulkeley's eyes searched the waters for PT 31, but he could wait no longer for the missing boat. He ordered the boat forward slowly on two engines. Ahead was the cruiser, and just as the Japanese searchlights locked on the Mosquito boat, it released two torpedoes.

"Hard rudder," Bulkeley commanded his quartermaster.

The little boat pulled out of there — fast! Looking over their shoulders, the crew members saw the first torpedo strike home. Two more explosions followed, as the enemy's powder magazines went up, taking the 6,000 ton cruiser with them.

The brave sailors cheered their success, but seconds later, the cheering stopped. They realized that only one of their torpedoes had fired. The other had stuck in the torpedo tube and was very much "alive." Even a wave might set it off. So despite the dangers around them, they were forced to stop and put the torpedo out of operation. Then, with engines wide open, the Mosquito boat roared out of Subic Bay.

Several days later, Bulkeley and his crew learned what had happened to PT 31. The small boat had gotten stuck on a reef. With the enemy all around, De Long decided to sink the boat and try to work his way back to the American lines. He and nine of his men managed to get back.

Things became worse for the American and Filipino soldiers in the days that followed, and General Douglas MacArthur, the Commander-in-Chief of the Pacific Theater of Operations, received orders to leave the Philippines and go to Australia. The

General didn't want to leave, but he had to obey orders. He selected Bulkeley's Mosquito boats for the first part of his journey, turning down the submarine that had been sent for that purpose. Bulkeley's boat carried the General, his wife, son, and Chinese nurse. The remaining PTs took others of the General's staff.

The enemy held practically all of the Philippines, so the trip was very dangerous. The Japanese controlled the air and the sea at this time, and the capture of General MacArthur would have been quite a prize for them.

The small boats left Corregidor on the night of March 11th. At 1900 hours (7 P.M.), Bulkeley in PT 41 and the rest of his squadron headed south toward the island of Mindinao five hundred miles away. They travelled by night and hid during the day. During their first stop, they were forced to abandon PT 32 because it ran out of fuel. Its passengers and crew crowded aboard Lieutenant Robert B. Kelly's PT 34. Then the small boats continued on their journey.

Finally, the Mosquito squadron reached the Mindinao Sea. Waves up to fifteen feet tossed the boats about like chips of wood. The sailors on deck were drenched to the skin, and passengers below were sick from the battering waters. Soon after, the sea calmed, and on the morning of the 13th, the PTs delivered their passengers to Cagayan on Mindinao. Unfortunately, the four American bombers that were supposed to meet the boats had run into difficulty, and the General and his party had to wait until March 18th for their flight to Australia.

Bulkeley and his squadron continued to strike at the enemy until April 10, 1942. They carried Philippine President Manuel Quezon to a bomber for a flight to Australia. Bulkeley himself fired two torpedoes into another Japanese cruiser. They struck and damaged the Japanese ship, but it took two more torpedoes fired by Kelly's PT 34 to sink the ship. Kelly's torpedoes were the last fired by the squadron. In the end, only one boat remained, but only one of the missing Mosquito boats had been destroyed by the enemy.

Since the PT crews were of no further use in the Philippines, General MacArthur brought as many of the men to Australia as he could. From there, they shipped back to the Motor Torpedo Boat Station at Mellville, Rhode Island, to train new crews. Among these new crews was a young officer named John F. Kennedy, who was later to carry on the tradition of the PTs. Still later, he was to become the 35th President of the United States.

For his heroism and leadership during those four months and eight days in Philippine waters, Lieutenant Commander Bulkeley received the Medal of Honor.

The Pirate of the Atlantic

During 1944, United States Naval Task Force
22.3 was under the command of the then Captain
Daniel V. Gallery. Captain Gallery's force con-
sisted of the aircraft carrier U.S.S. *Guadalcanal*,
and five speedy destroyer escorts — the *Pillsbury,
Chatelaine, Jenks, Pope,* and *Flaherty.*

The task force's job was to protect American and
allied troop supply ships crossing the Atlantic. It
wasn't an easy job. Captain Gallery's men had to
defend against enemy raids from the skies and
beneath the seas. In addition, his force had to seek
and destroy enemy submarines, as hundreds of
Nazi U-boats beneath the Atlantic continually
threatened all ship movements.

By spring 1944, Task Force 22.3 had sunk 3
U-boats, but Captain Gallery wasn't satisfied. Each
sinking had followed a pattern. First the sub, damaged by depth charges, would surface quickly to let

its crew escape. Then the sub would be scuttled and sink to the bottom, for good. Captain Gallery figured that if an American crew were put aboard a damaged sub immediately after it surfaced, it might be saved.

In order to carry out his plan for capturing such a prize, Captain Gallery ordered his destroyer escort captains to train boarding parties and keep their whaleboats uncovered on alert status.

On June 4, 1944, Captain Gallery got a chance to put his plan into operation.

For more than a week, Task Force 22.3 had been tracking an enemy sub about 150 miles off the coast of French West Africa. Then the force caught up with the crafty U-boat.

On board the *Chatelaine*, the sonar operator picked up an unidentified ping in his headset. Then he fixed the ping's location, and the *Chatelaine*, after alerting the rest of the force, sped at full steam to the area indicated.

The entire force followed and two fighter planes took off from the deck of the *Guadalcanal*. The planes soon spotted a sub silhouette beneath the waves and relayed that information to the ships below.

Circling rapidly, the *Chatelaine* dropped a deadly pattern of depth charges. Loaded with explosives, these depth charges resemble large ash cans, and when the charges detonate near a sub, the shock waves produced in the water can rupture the sub's plates and damage her controls. After some anxious moments, the *Chatelaine's* barrage struck its mark.

Below the surface of the sea, Harold Lange, the German sub commander, had his hands full. The depth charges had jammed the rudder of his sub, the U-505. Without controls and suffering from other damage, the U-505 had little chance to escape. "Bring her up to the surface," Lieutenant Lange ordered, "and make ready to abandon."

As the U-505 broke the surface, its crew members started jumping overboard to escape the fire of the task force deck guns and torpedoes. The last men off the sub dutifully opened its seacocks to let in the ocean. A little more than 500 yards from the surfaced U-505 sat the *Chatelaine*.

Seeing the closeness of the sub to the *Chatelaine* and his other ships, Captain Gallery decided that he might have a chance to capture the damaged U-505. "Cease fire!" he commanded the force, and when the ships had stopped firing, he called, "Boarders away!"

The command "Boarders away!" had not been used by a U.S. Naval Commander in over a century. Once sailors had swung from their ship's rigging onto the deck of an enemy ship for hand-to-hand battle, but that kind of naval engagement had disappeared with the sailing ship. Nevertheless, on June 4, 1944, Captain Gallery issued that almost forgotten order.

Commanded by Lieutenant Junior Grade Albert David, the *Pillsbury's* whaleboat reached the lurching U-505 first. A native of Maryville, Maryland, Lieutenant David had entered the navy as an enlisted man and worked up to an officer's commission. Now within striking distance of the German sub, he faced the most important decision of his naval career.

Because of her damaged rudder, the sub was turning in circles. Meanwhile the sea was pouring down her open hatches and up through her seacocks. No one could tell if the sub was about to upend and sink below the waves forever. And for a final threat, there was always the possibility that some armed Germans might have remained aboard the sub.

"Come on," Lieutenant David said, leaping onto the sub's slippery, heaving deck. "She's not going to wait for us."

Seconds later, he and his men scrambled down the hatches, which they secured behind them, to close the valves. Then the determined whaleboat crew set to work on the almost flooded sub.

While the lieutenant and his men worked feverishly inside the U-505, the *Pillsbury* swung alongside and tossed a line aboard in an attempt to take the sub in tow. A wave then slammed the U-505, and the captured sub lashed out, almost as if in a final attack, into the side of the *Pillsbury*. The sub's sharp bow planes cut into the thin steel plates of the *Pillsbury* and flooded two of her compartments.

The *Guadalcanal* then sent a second boarding party which succeeded in securing a tow line from the carrier to the sub. Two weeks later, Task Force 22.3 steamed into Bermuda, the U-505 in tow, as a prize of war.

Naval intelligence men quickly broke the U-505's codebooks, and knowledge of these codes helped U.S. ships to sink 290 U-boats during the remaining ten months of the war. By comparison, a total of 781 German subs were sunk by U.S. and allied ships in the entire war.

For this day's work, Task Force 22.3 received a Presidential Unit Citation. In addition, each member of the *Pillsbury's* boarding party received a medal in recognition of his courageous action. The party's leader, Lieutenant David, received his nation's highest military award — the Medal of Honor. This was the only one awarded for the battle of the Atlantic, and his capture of the U-505 marked the first boarding and capture of an enemy man-o'-war on the high seas by the U.S. Navy since 1815.

For many years now, the U-505 has been on permanent exhibit in Chicago's Museum of Science and Industry, and hundreds of thousands of visitors to the museum have walked through and inspected the captured sub. It is a prize of war, but more than that, it is a monument to the brave officers and men of Task Force 22.3.

KOREA

Hero with a Personal Grudge

Most men probably go off to war with one thought in mind — staying alive. Until the first bombs or bullets explode nearby, the enemy probably seems unreal, but those first explosions make it clear that killing the enemy is necessary for staying alive. For Ronald E. Rosser, killing the enemy was always more important than staying alive.

In 1946, Ronald quit high school and enlisted in the army. When his three-year enlistment was over, he returned to his hometown of Crooksville, Ohio, and got a job at the Misco mines.

The United States went to war in Korea the following year. To most Americans, Korea meant very little. It was a relatively small country in Southeast Asia, and it posed no real threat to the American public. Many people even questioned the United States' involvement in the war.

To Ronald and his fourteen brothers and sisters,

the war became personal when Ronald's younger brother, Dick, was sent to Korea. Then in February 1951, the war became a personal tragedy to the Rossers when they received the word that Dick had been killed by the Red Chinese.

The news hurt each member of the family, and Ronald decided that he was going to avenge his brother's death. That night, he told his father, "Dad, I'm going back in, and I'm going to make them pay for what they did to Dick."

Ronald reenlisted the next day and soon shipped out to the Far East Command. In Korea, he earned the rank of corporal and served as a forward observer for the 38th Infantry Regiment.

Then on January 12, 1952, Ronald and Corporal Stanley Smith, another forward observer, received orders to report to Company L of the 38th Infantry. The company's orders were to destroy an enemy hill position.

It wasn't an easy assignment. Going uphill at enemy guns is never easy, and this particular enemy position had a large number of men and weapons to defend it. Ronald and Corporal Smith had key roles. They had to move up with the first platoon in the assault, pinpoint the enemy's position, and radio that information back so that the heavy mortar would be prepared to fire when called into action.

Determined to score a victory, the platoon moved quickly up the hill and was about 100 yards from the enemy position before the Chinese Reds' heavy automatic weapons stopped the advance. Pinned down with the others, Ronald couldn't choke off thoughts of his younger brother and of the desire for revenge that had brought him to Southeast Asia.

He handed his radio to Smith. Then he rushed up toward the enemy position, carrying a carbine rifle and a white phosphorous grenade. Not once did he hesitate, though mortar shells and rifle fire ripped and shattered the ground around him.

After firing into the first enemy bunker, he leaped over it onto the edge of a trench. On each side of him, a Chinese soldier rose and prepared to fire at Ronald. He was ready for them, drilling one through the head and turning fast enough to fire a second round into the chest of the other.

Leaping down into the trench, Ronald had no time to think about the two Chinese soldiers who had just paid for his brother's death, because the trench was alive with soldiers who were turning their weapons on him. He raced at their positions, firing bursts from his carbine and killing five of them.

Then Ronald noticed a sixth man crawling into a bunker at the end of the trench. Realizing that the bunker could be filled with enemy soldiers, Ronald moved cautiously to the bunker opening and tossed his grenade into it. Seconds later, the grenade exploded, and two more Red soldiers came charging out of the bunker. Ronald's carbine dropped both of them.

He raced back down the hill for ammunition, and this time, several other soldiers followed him on a charge back up to the top. Again, the charge was through enemy fire, and though some soldiers were hit, Ronald reached the top. "Come on!" he called to the others.

With Ronald in the lead, they raced from bunker to bunker, hurling grenades and following up with carbine fire. Ronald got hit slightly on the hand, but he continued his race to the bunkers until his ammunition was gone.

After Ronald's final trip down and up the hill, word came for the company to group up and withdraw. The enemy position had been reduced enough so that it would no longer present a major threat.

To avenge his brother's death, Ronald had killed thirteen Red soldiers. He thought about that as a medical aidman patched the slight hand wound he had received during the assault.

Men who had observed Ronald's daring deeds recommended that he be given the Medal of Honor, and a short time later, he journeyed to Washington to receive the award. On that day, a bus paid for and chartered by the Misco mine and its employees left Crooksville bound for Washington and the award ceremonies.

He Refused to Quit

Cornelius "Connie" Charlton was the eighth of seventeen children born to Mr. and Mrs. Van Charlton. When Connie was twelve years old, the United States was in the midst of World War II, and Connie's brothers were serving in the Marines and Army.

Connie admired their uniforms, and three years later he begged his mother to let him enlist in the army. His mother refused, reminding him that her children did not lie about their age or anything else. In 1946, Connie became old enough to enlist, and his mother agreed to let him go.

Connie liked the army as much as he had expected, and after basic training, he was sent to Germany. While there, he reenlisted. "Well, if anyone wanted to talk me out of staying in the army," he said while home on leave, "it's too late now. Maybe that's why I reenlisted over there."

Then early in 1950, Connie received orders assigning him to the Far East Command. It was a time of peace, but recent actions of the North Korean Army indicated that South Korea could be plunged into war at any time. Connie shipped over to Okinawa and served there with an engineering battalion.

On June 25, 1950, the uneasy peace in Korea came to an end. Battle units of the North Korean Army crossed the Parallel dividing the two countries. Two days later, President Harry S Truman commanded United States armed forces to support the South Koreans. Connie's battalion was among the first to touch the soil in South Korea.

Connie made sergeant in 1951. The war was getting rougher every day, but Connie's outfit worked many miles behind the front lines. Then one day, Connie asked for a transfer to the Twenty-fourth Infantry Regiment. The Twenty-fourth was fighting the Chinese in the hills of South Korea.

"You must be kidding," Connie's commanding officer said. "You're coming up for another promotion, so why do you want to take a chance on losing it by transferring?"

"Well, that's what I want to do," Connie said.

The Twenty-fourth was the army's last segregated outfit. Its combat record wasn't good, and the black men in the outfit showed no great enthusiasm for it. Perhaps they didn't like being separated by race. Perhaps Connie didn't like the stories that he heard about the Twenty-fourth. Perhaps he decided that if any of his people were separated because of their color, he should be separated with them. Or perhaps he just wanted to fight. In any event, he got his transfer to the Twenty-fourth.

Connie joined C Company of the Twenty-fourth Regiment in March of 1951. He was only twenty-one years old, but he was over six feet tall and knew how to handle men. When he talked, the men in his platoon listened.

From March until late May, the regiment was pushed back by advancing enemy troops. Then the Chinese were stopped, and the Twenty-fourth began a push northward.

Connie's platoon reached Hill 543 on June 1. A large enemy force held the hill, so Connie and the lieutenant in charge of the platoon each took half of the men. One group would advance, while the other group would provide cover fire. Minutes later, the lieutenant fell dead from enemy fire. Connie quickly regrouped the platoon and moved to the front. He was in charge, and heavy enemy fire had his entire platoon pinned down.

Taking another note of enemy gun positions, Connie said, "A few of you men follow me. We're going to take out that first gun up there."

As Connie and the three or four men who followed him neared the enemy, the blast of a grenade knocked him down. Shaking his head, he scrambled to his feet and heaved a grenade into the hole which concealed the Red soldiers. After the grenade exploded, a few enemy soldiers came out of the hole and Connie dropped them with his carbine.

Once again, Connie regrouped the men remaining in his platoon and led them up the rugged hillside toward an enemy machine gun position. Then a Red grenade tore a hole in Connie's chest.

"You're hit bad, Sarge," one of Connie's men said. "Here, let me see if I can patch you up."

"There's no time for that," Connie answered. "I want the men with bad wounds to keep down and wait for medical treatment. Or wait until we can get you off this hill. The rest of you follow me."

This time, they made it through the hail of fire coming down on them and reached the top of the hill. Spotting an enemy machine gun, Connie waved his men off and went at it alone. Just before he reached the gun, another grenade ripped into his body, but he kept going and silenced the Reds and their gun. Then he fell dead.

Later that day, the Chinese counterattacked and took the hill again for a short time. Nevertheless, Connie and his men had severely weakened the enemy, and another American unit took the hill without a battle. From then on, the hill was known as Charlton Hill.

On Lincoln's birthday in 1952, President Harry S Truman awarded Sergeant Cornelius H. Charlton's Medal of Honor to his parents. Sad but proud, Mr. and Mrs. Van Charlton listened as the President praised the brave deeds of their son.

Ironically enough, less than sixty days after Connie's death, on July 26, 1951, the Twenty-fourth Infantry Regiment was disbanded. Commenting on that occasion, Eighth Army Commander General Matthew B. Ridgeway said, "It has been satisfactorily demonstrated that in combat in Korea Negro soldiers serve more effectively in integrated units."

Prisoner of War

On July 27, 1953, North Korean and United Nation forces signed an armistice ending the Korean War. Both sides exchanged many prisoners a few months later. One of the American prisoners exchanged was so thin that he was barely recognizable. He had been a prisoner for over three years, and he had gone through experiences that only a very strong man could survive. He was General William Frische Dean, Commanding Officer of the 24th Infantry Division.

"Bill" Dean was born in Carlyle, Illinois. As a young man, he dreamed of going to West Point, but when he failed the entrance examination, he offered no excuses. Instead he entered the University of California and worked his way through school, taking many different jobs during his four years.

After graduation, Bill received a second lieuten-

ant's commission and entered the Army in 1923. When the Japanese bombed Pearl Harbor eighteen years later, Bill Dean was a little-known major, but wartime, unfortunately, is the best time for promotions in the Army. So by the end of World War II, Bill Dean had climbed to the rank of two-star general, and he had gotten the reputation of being a man who took too many chances — with his own life. A general was supposed to stay in the rear and do the planning, but General Dean liked to be where the action was.

Less than five years after the close of World War II, July 4, 1950, General Dean got another chance to be near the action. He arrived in Korea with his 24th Infantry Division. For the next two weeks, the 24th tried to keep the enemy busy, while the U.S. Eighth Army unloaded and readied its defenses around Pusan, South Korea.

Then on July 19, the North Koreans set their sights on Dean's Division which was north of the town of Taejon. Enemy artillery banged away at the 24th to soften it up for the attack that was sure to follow. Then General Dean received orders from the Commander of the United Nations Forces, General Douglas MacArthur. They read: "Urgent that you hold Taejon for two more days."

By morning, at least two North Korean Divisions were attacking Dean's badly outnumbered troops. Nevertheless, General Dean determined that he still could follow his orders. He sent most of the Division south to set up a defensive position and wait for his orders, while he stayed behind with parts of the 19th and 34th Infantry Regiments, hoping to keep the enemy busy for two days.

Still willing to take chances with his life, Dean plunged right into action, leading bazooka teams in attacks on enemy tanks and scouting targets for air strikes. He and the brave infantrymen that had remained in Taejon held the town for three days. Their heroic actions saved Pusan from almost certain enemy destruction, and this marked a turning point in the Korean War.

When General Dean finally ordered an all-out retreat, massive enemy forces had the burning town surrounded. Loading into all the remaining vehicles, the American troops started down a narrow road that led to Pusan. One of the last vehicles in the retreating column was General Dean's jeep.

For four miles, the column inched its way through enemy rifle, machine gun, and mortar fire, but as the toll of stalled and damaged trucks and jeeps mounted, it became impossible to get through on the narrow road. Then General Dean and about twenty other men started for Pusan on foot. Dean figured the darkness of night that was closing in would help them avoid the enemy.

Still the darkness hampered Dean and the others, as they struggled down the road, taking chances carrying the wounded and trying to keep together. When they passed near a mountain stream, the General fell behind the others to get some water for himself and one of the wounded men.

Nearing the stream, Dean lost his footing on the steep embankment and tumbled down it. He landed on his head and lost consciousness. A short time later, some men noticed that the General hadn't returned, so the entire group started to search for him. The darkness and the closeness of enemy troops proved too much of an obstacle for the searchers, and one officer reluctantly told them, "We've got to push on without General Dean. I can't tell what happened to him, but let's hope that he's all right."

About four hours after his fall, Dean regained consciousness. Only slightly aware of what had happened to him, he took a drink from the stream and fell off into sleep for another four hours.

Awakening again near dawn, Bill Dean lifted his pain-filled, weary body and started out for what he hoped would be the American lines. His fall had broken his left shoulder and severely bruised the rest of his body.

Dean staggered around for a week trying to find United Nation lines before he realized that he was lost, but the sounds of fighting nearby gave him courage to continue his search for help. He ate what he could find — raw rice, wild berries — and the weight fell off his once strong 210-pound body.

Occasionally Dean begged a meal from Korean farmers, but he knew that the farmers might turn him in to the enemy, so he ate and ran. By the middle of his fourth week behind enemy lines, he weighed about 150 pounds.

Then one morning, he ran into Lieutenant Stanley Tabor of the 19th Infantry Regiment. Tabor, who was also lost, was shocked to see another American, especially the General in charge of his division. For a short time, the two men compared their experiences. Then they headed south.

The following night, Tabor spotted a farmhouse and said to Dean, "Let's stop there for a meal. We can't go on without food."

Tabor had a carbine and Dean had a forty-five, so the two men could have kept watch on the farmhouse's occupants, nevertheless Dean said, "No, it's too risky."

After a few more days, Dean finally agreed that they would have to stop at a farmhouse for food. Up to that time, he had had about six real meals in four weeks. That night they entered a farmhouse, and the Korean inside offered them food.

Minutes later, rifle shots slammed into the house, and enemy soldiers called for Dean and Tabor to surrender. The two Americans raced out of a rear door and plunged into some rain-filled rice paddies. The two men managed to escape successfully, but they lost each other in the darkness and were on their own once again. Dean also lost the use of his forty-five when it became too wet and wouldn't fire.

Dean continued on, though now he was so weak that he willingly had to trust anyone who offered help. Finally, on Dean's thirty-fifth day behind enemy lines, August 25, 1950, a young Korean turned him over to enemy soldiers for a reward of five dollars.

The American General was a big prize for the North Koreans, and they questioned him hour after hour, day after day. Once, the North Koreans questioned Dean for almost three days without a break, but he refused to give them anything more than his name, rank, serial number and date of birth.

For five months, General Dean sat only in his underwear on the cold floor of a room kept just at the freezing level, while his North Korean captors promised everything from steaks to torture in hopes of making him talk or make statements condemning his country. Despite all this, Bill Dean steadfastly refused to offer even a shred of information and, in the end, the North Koreans decided to leave him alone. Perhaps they admired his courage. Or perhaps they concluded that the man would never talk. Whatever the case, Bill Dean, now 105 pounds, would spend the rest of his confinement free of the pressures that characterized his first five months in North Korean hands.

Meanwhile, back in the United States, military leaders held little hope for General Dean. His body was missing, and his helmet liner had been found near Taejon with a bullet hole in it. For his action in holding Taejon, Dean had been recommended for the Medal of Honor, and during the winter of 1951, President Harry S Truman awarded the Medal to Dean's wife.

In September 1953, Bill Dean came back from the "dead" in a prisoner exchange with North Korea. To himself, he was no hero, but to the millions of Americans who read his story in newspapers, he was a hero of the highest order.

A new president, General Dwight D. Eisenhower, personally presented General William Dean with his Medal of Honor, and then the fifty-four-year-old warrior retired.

During the Korean War, many American soldiers "cooperated" with the enemy after being taken prisoner. Bill Dean had more reason than most to give his captors what they wanted, but he remained true to his country and — most of all — to himself.

VIETNAM

Man in a Green Beret

Roger Donlon grew up in Saurguties, New York. There he first showed signs of leadership and courage, being elected president of his junior class in high school and playing end on the football team. Later, he spent almost two years at West Point, and shortly after leaving the military academy, he enlisted in the army.

The following year, in June 1959, he graduated from Officer Candidate School at Fort Benning, Georgia, and received his commission as an infantry second lieutenant. Then Roger went on to airborne training. After that, he served as an airborne officer in Alaska and South Carolina.

Planning to make the army his career, he then enrolled in the United States Army Special Warfare School, Fort Bragg, North Carolina. Here he would undergo some of the most rugged training offered in any branch of the armed forces, and upon completion he would be a member of the famous "Green Berets."

He knew what he faced. An army pamphlet described the training this way: —

"When you're a Special Forces soldier, you must be able to move into any area, under every conceivable condition. This is why all Special Forces men must be Airborne-qualified. This is why they all know how to swim. This is why they must be in top shape all the time. This is why they must be able to climb mountains, to traverse snow, to move efficiently through jungle undergrowth. You can expect to get all this training and more when you are a Special Forces soldier. You'll know how to jump from airplanes or helicopters. You'll know how to rappel down the side of a sheer cliff. You'll know how to paddle a raft up an alligator-infested river. When you are a Special Forces soldier you and your mission can be anywhere in the world and nothing can stop you from getting to the place where you're needed."

And once you're there...

"It could be far from civilization. But wherever it is, your Special Forces training keeps you going for as long as you have to. All Special Forces soldiers are trained to live off the land. You'll know how to trap animals. You'll know which plants are poisonous. You'll know how to handle dangerous snakes. You'll know how to camouflage yourself so that your best friend couldn't see you at two yards. And you'll be an expert at evading your pursuers and escaping capture. Not only will you know all this: You will also have to teach it to the people you work with. Don't forget, the people you will be sent to help will look up to you and expect the impossible from you. Your Special Forces training and your on-the-job experience will see to it that their hopes are justified."

Roger successfully completed the training, and a short time later, he was given the command of a Special Forces unit to be stationed in Viet Nam for the purpose of advising and training units of the South Vietnamese Army. For Roger, now a captain, and the eleven men assigned to him, South Vietnam would provide a true test of their Special Forces training.

Captain Donlon and his men went to Nam Dong, a camp close to the borders of Laos and North Viet Nam. There they served as advisors to 311 South Vietnamese soldiers. In addition, Kevin Conway, an Australian warrant officer, also advised the camp's native defenders.

In the early hours of the morning of July 6, 1964, Viet Cong soldiers worked their way through the dark jungles near Camp Nam Dong. Usually, the Viet Cong moved in small guerrilla bands, but this time they came as a battalion of 900 fighting men, well-armed with Red Chinese and Soviet mortars, grenades, rifles, and other small arms including a good supply of U.S. weapons taken in combat from the South Vietnamese.

The first mortar round, a blazing ball of white phosphorus, rocked the sleeping camp. Seconds later, more and more high explosive and white phosphorus shells and grenades thundered down on the camp. The VC were finding their targets.

Thatched roofs were going up like torches. In the light of the burning buildings, men scurried about in all stages of dress and undress, grabbing for their weapons and heading for their posts.

Captain Donlon moved swiftly to direct the fire of his men against the enemy now swarming around the area. As he looked about, he noticed a blaze in the command post. The building which housed weapons, ammunition, radios, and other equipment was burning like a bonfire. Some of his men joined him in the race to the building.

Quickly they removed ammo and supplies. Several times, mortar blasts flipped Captain Donlon into the air, and first one shoe was torn off his foot, then the other. Then in stocking feet he rushed for the main gate to stop an enemy breakthrough. As he ran, bullets sliced the air all around him. Grenades exploded, but he continued toward the figures he had spotted.

Near the gate he saw the three enemy guerrillas setting a dynamite charge. Without waiting for aid, he attacked the enemy, opening up with his rifle and killing two of them. He then pulled the pin from a grenade and lobbed it at the third dynamiter who was crawling away. The man and his explosives went up together.

He rushed on toward one of his own mortar positions, and just before he reached it, fragments of steel tore into his stomach. Stuffing a piece of his torn shirt into the wound, he crawled on his hands and knees into the position.

There he found that most of the men in the crew had been wounded. "There's no sense in trying to hold this position. Move out," he said. "I'll cover you."

The men withdrew, except for the sergeant commanding their position. He was badly wounded, so Captain Donlon threw the man's arm over his shoulder and dragged the wounded man toward safety. Then an enemy mortar shell burst, practically on top of them. The captain landed more than five yards away with a wound in his left shoulder. The sergeant was dead.

Captain Donlon had been trained well for he did not stop. Finding an abandoned mortar, he carried it thirty yards to a crew in another position. There he found three men wounded and bandaged them with pieces of his T shirt. A small remaining piece he stuffed into his own stomach wound and then moved on. He dodged enemy fire two more times to save abandoned weapons and ammo, and though he managed to stay alive, he received his third wound — grenade fragments in the leg.

The pain ate into all parts of his body, but the battle was not over. He crawled hundreds of yards, checking gun positions and guard posts and shouting words of encouragement to his men. Then another mortar explosion sent slivers of steel into his face and body.

The captain was a bloody mess, but he wasn't through yet. He got on the radio to guide the planes from Da Nang that were dropping flares to light up the VC's positions so that his men could see their targets.

Finally, the morning sun broke through. The VC retreated into the jungle, leaving behind fifty-four dead. The five-hour battle was over, and Camp Nam Dong was saved.

Of Donlon's men, two were dead along with the Australian warrant officer, and seven were wounded, but ten of the original twelve green berets were still alive, and this certainly was, in part, a tribute to their training.

Captain Donlon quickly reorganized the defense of the camp in case of another enemy attack. Then seeing that all his men had been treated, he accepted the medical aid that he had been refusing.

On December 5, 1964, President Lyndon Johnson awarded the Medal of Honor to Roger Donlon in a ceremony at the White House. Captain Donlon was the first man to win the award for action in Viet Nam.

They Called Him "Preacher"

On November 7, 1946, Clara Lee Olive died while giving birth to a son. Her son was named Milton Olive III, and he grew up on Chicago's South Side.

After Milton's third year of high school, he wanted to join the army. "You're only seventeen years old," his father told him. "The army can wait another year for you. Finish school first."

"I don't want to finish school," Milton said. "I want to enlist, Dad."

In August 1964, one month before the start of Milton's senior year in high school, he enlisted in the army for three years. Then he left for his basic combat training at Fort Knox, Kentucky.

Milton was trained to be a communications specialist right after his basic training, but he still had some other training in mind. On leave, he told his father, "I signed up for the paratroopers."

Milton's father could see that his son was proud of his uniform, and he thought that perhaps Milton would make a career of military service. He knew that a young man without a high school diploma would find it difficult to make a living in civilian life, especially a young black man.

The Basic Airborne Course at Fort Benning, Georgia is rough, because any man who parachutes from a plane must be in top mental and physical condition. Many men fail to make it through the training period, but Milton wanted the Parachutist Badge. In May 1965, he finished the course and proudly attached the badge to his uniform.

Almost immediately, Milton left for Viet Nam with the 173rd Airborne Brigade, and in July he fought in his first battle and was wounded. By then, his buddies had started calling him "Preacher," because he was fond of quoting the Bible to them, and they were glad that Milton's wound was slight.

"Preacher, when they give you your Purple Heart," one buddy told Milton, "you'd better send it home. You'll lose it crawling around these jungles."

Not wishing to create worries at home, Milton kept the medal and his wound secret. He tried to make his letters cheerful as possible, but the deadly seriousness of war always seemed to show through. On October 22, 1965, he wrote, "We all do a man's job and wear a man's clothes and call ourselves men, but some of us are still little boys."

Five days later, Milton's platoon was on a search and destroy mission in the jungle near Phu Cuong. Heavy enemy gun fire pinned down the platoon.

Then Milton and the others charged the Viet Cong gun positions. Deciding to flee, enemy soldiers raced off into the jungle, and Milton's platoon followed after them.

Milton and four other soldiers moved cautiously through the thicket. They were prepared for more trouble, but they weren't prepared for the grenade that fell into their midst. Soldiers might, at one time or another, think about what they would do in the few seconds before the grenade explodes, but they can never prepare for the event.

"Look out, Hop!" Milton called to Specialist Fourth Class John Foster. Then before anyone could reply, Milton grabbed the grenade and fell on it. Milton's body absorbed the blast that followed, and the four other men were saved.

On April 21, 1966, President Johnson presented Private First Class Olive's Medal of Honor to the dead soldier's father. Two men, First Lieutenant Jimmy Stanford and Specialist Foster, stood nearby, listening to the President and thinking of the day when "Preacher" gave his life for them.

Toward the end of his remarks in the White House Rose Garden, President Johnson noted that Milton was the eighth Negro American to receive the Medal of Honor. "Fortunately," the President explained, "it will be more difficult for future Presidents to say how many Negroes have received the Medal of Honor, for unlike the other seven, Private Olive's military records have never carried the color of his skin or his racial origin, only the testimony that he was a good and loyal citizen of the United States of America."

Unarmed Hero

Lawrence Joel was born in Winston-Salem, North Carolina. When he was eight years old, in 1936, he had to leave home. Lawrence's parents were too poor to care for him, so they gave him to Mr. and Mrs. Clayton Samuel. The Samuels became Lawrence's foster parents, and they raised him along with their five daughters.

Lawrence finished high school in 1945, and the next year he enlisted in the army for three years. During those years, he took paratrooper training and served in Italy. He liked the army, but when his enlistment ended, he decided to return to civilian life. After four years of civilian life, he reenlisted, planning then to make the army his career.

He returned to the paratroopers and soon received training as a medical aidman. In this role, Lawrence Joel, a specialist five, went to Viet Nam with the 1st Airborne Battalion, 503rd Infantry, early in 1965.

On November 8, 1965, Specialist Joel's Company was attacked by the Viet Cong. The enemy force was large and well-hidden in the heavy foliage common throughout Viet Nam. Joel saw that the lead squad had been hit heavily by the rifle and machine gun fire. He rushed forward to treat and help evacuate the wounded.

"It's only a scratch," Joel told one wounded man who looked worried. "You're lucky"

While Joel patched the wounded, the battle continued and men from his company moved into the positions that they had been ordered to take. Once again, the heavy enemy gun fire killed and wounded many men.

Joel moved forward, treating the wounded as he went. Then machine gun bullets tore into his right leg, and he rolled over from the force of the bullets and the pain. He looked down. The leg was a bloody mess, but it was all there.

Quickly, he tore away the bits of olive cloth still remaining on his right leg and bandaged it. The pain ran through his body, as he listened to the cries of the wounded. "Stay cool," he called. "I'll be right there."

Then he reached into his medical supplies for a needle of morphine. The morphine would deaden his pain and give him a chance to work on the wounded. He jabbed the needle into his skin, hoping the pain-killing morphine would ease his pain quickly.

"Stay down," another soldier called to Joel, "the Cong can see you."

Other soldiers also called to him, but Joel would

not listen. Again, he moved forward, seeking the wounded. He found one man who lost a lot of blood. He realized the man needed fresh blood immediately.

Bullets ripped into the ground around Joel, but he came up to a kneeling position, holding the plasma bottles high so that the blood would flow into the man's veins.

After that, he moved on. Then enemy fire hit him again, and a bullet stuck in his thigh. Slowly, he dragged himself across the battlefield, bandaging and treating thirteen more men before his medical supplies ran out.

Unwilling to stop and seek treatment for his own wounds, he sent word to the rear that he was out of supplies. Then he continued his search for wounded men.

Joel crawled over to a man gushing blood from a chest wound. Realizing that the man would bleed to death before the supplies arrived, Joel placed a plastic bag over the wound, hoping that the bag would stop the flow of blood. For a brief moment, Joel feared that his effort had failed, but then the blood stopped. The man was saved.

Finally, a man with new medical supplies reached Joel. "Man, you'd better pull back," he told Joel. "Look at your leg."

"It's all right," Joel replied, checking his fresh supplies.

Then he crawled off through gun fire which peppered the earth around him. The battle raged on for twenty-four hours, and Joel continued crawling and calling, "Stay loose, pal. I'll be there."

Even after the battle ended, Viet Cong snipers continued to halt the free movement of dead and wounded. American losses were heavy, and the elusive Viet Cong left four hundred and ten dead behind. Finally, an officer told Joel, "Specialist, I want you to pull back and get that leg patched up now, and that's an order."

The courageous 39-year old medic was promoted, and on March 9, 1967, he stood on the White House lawn flanked by President Johnson and Vice President Humphrey. Specialist Sixth Class Lawrence Joel listened to the 21-gun salute honoring him, listened as Army Secretary Stanley R. Resor read the citation for Joel's Medal of Honor, and listened as President Johnson said, "As we salute the valor of this soldier, we salute the best in the American tradition."

Mr. and Mrs. Clayton Samuel, Lawrence Joel's foster parents, stood nearby. They had raised a man — an unarmed hero.

Eighth Cavalry Machine Gunner

David Dolby graduated from Spring-Ford High School, Ryorsford, Pennsylvania in 1964. On February 3 of the following year, he enlisted in the army for three years. He wanted to be a paratrooper, so after his basic combat training, he attended the Basic Airborne Course at Fort Benning, Georgia.

Three months later, in August 1965, David went to South Viet Nam with Company B, 1st Airborne Battalion, of the Eighth Cavalry. So by the time the fateful day of May 21, 1966, arrived, David had seen plenty of action, had spent some time in a hospital on Okinawa recovering from a slight wound, and had attained the rank of specialist four.

The army called it Operation Crazy Horse. For David, one-week past his twentieth birthday, that meant that his platoon had to take a ridge near An Khe.

As the men of the 1st Platoon moved out single-file, David thought about their assignment. He guessed that they were going to run into more than the usual snipers because other units had been to the ridge before and had reported that it was a very strong enemy position.

David and the three other men in his machine gun crew were in the middle of the file as it started for the top of the hill. Then a short burst of enemy fire from the right sent the men diving for cover. They waited for more fire, but when none came, they guessed that it was only a sniper and started to move up.

Then the platoon was hit again. This time, it was heavy fire and it came from all directions. David spotted two machine gun bunkers right above him, and one on the ridge behind him. He also saw many platoon members falling.

David started moving up the hill, firing his M-60 machine gun. He was a difficult target for the enemy. He had his face coated with camouflage paint and twigs and branches tied all over his body. Nevertheless, bullets tatooed the ground around him.

He continued his upward climb until he located an enemy machine gun bunker. It wasn't one of the two that he had seen from below. They were still some distance away, but this new bunker had to be silenced.

Approaching from the side, David surprised the three enemy soldiers manning the gun and dropped all of them with one short burst. Then he spotted another bunker to his right, and three more enemy soldiers fell dead.

After killing a lone rifleman in a hole, he stopped and tried to find the rifleman who had been firing at him repeatedly. The bullets had been getting closer and closer, and David knew that it had to be the man or him. Finally, he saw the man in a tree and downed him.

Then David realized that the two bunkers above him hadn't fired for a while. Maybe the men in them were dead? Or maybe they were waiting for some better shots at David? He wasn't going to try to find out by himself, so he moved back down the hill to get some help.

He soon reached his platoon leader, but before David could ask for help, enemy fire sprayed the area. One round skipped off David's helmet, and he moved back out of the line of fire. The lieutenant in charge of the platoon wasn't as lucky as David. A round seriously wounded him.

A short time later, a man found David and said, "The lieutenant wants to see you, Dolby, and you'd better hurry. He's in bad shape."

David rushed over, and the wounded platoon leader told him, "One of them got me good, Dolby. You're going to have to take over. Do the best you can, but if you have to move back, make sure you take all of our men with you." Then he slipped into unconsciousness.

David glanced at the men near the top of the hill. They were pinned down by the enemy machine guns. Finding a radio-telephone operator, David put a call through to B Company's Commander and explained that he was now in charge of his platoon. Then he said, "I think we're going to need some helicopter support so those guys who are pinned down can pull back."

"They're on the way," David's CO answered. "When they get close, pop some smoke onto the enemy position."

"Yes, sir!" David said, hearing the roar of the helicopters' engines.

Then David signaled his assistant gunner to unload a smoke grenade. It landed perfectly on one of the enemy positions, and the gunships began to pound away with aerial rocket artillery. At the same time, the men near the top of the hill started to pull back.

Taking the phone again, David told his CO, "They made fine hits, sir, but on their next pass, they're going to have to put their rockets a little higher up on the ridge. There's another line of bunkers up there."

"Can do," the CO said, "but you'll have to give the air boys some smoke to fire at."

David knew that he was too far away from the air strike target to put a smoke grenade on it, and the only way to get closer to it was to silence a nearby enemy machine gun harrassing him and his men. Slowly, he worked his way to within range of the enemy gun. From behind a tree, he saw that two men were on the gun. Then they spotted him, but before they could fire at him, they were dead.

When David reached the bottom of the ridge again, the radio-telephone operator said, "They want more smoke."

Feeling that the area was now somewhat safe, David rushed a short distance up the hill and tossed a smoke grenade. The hill was very steep, and the grenade came rolling back down it. David picked it up and heaved it to the rear of his own position. "Call them quick and tell them not to pay any attention to that smoke!" he screamed to the radio-telephone operator.

Once again, the helicopters started coming in. David watched their first hits. Then he called and helped them get a better line on the target. This time the aerial rockets didn't miss.

Darkness and heavy monsoon rains settled on the area at almost the same time. "I think we're going to be all right," David told his CO.

"Well, try to hold the position," the CO said. "I'm with the 2nd Platoon now. We're trying to get around there to help you."

David and his men waited. Then another call came from the CO, telling them to move back.

The platoon started its withdrawal. Most of the wounded could move under their own power. Others were helped. Only one man had to be carried. He was lifted onto David's back, and they began their return trip. Later that night, the man David carried back died.

Fortunately, many other men were saved because of the actions of Specialist Dolby, and on September 28, 1967, he received the Medal of Honor from President Johnson in ceremonies at the White House. At that time, the 21-year-old soldier from Oaks, Pennsylvania became the youngest living Medal of Honor winner.

Helicopter Rescue Pilot

Gerald Young was born in Chicago, Illinois, but before he started school, his family moved to Colorado Springs, Colorado. There he grew up, and at the age of seventeen, he enlisted in the Navy Reserve.

The following year, 1948, he went on active duty for four years, serving part of that time during the Korean War. Then in 1952, he returned to Colorado and took a civilian job at Peterson Air Force Base. At the same time, he used the benefits from his G.I. Bill to learn how to fly.

When Gerald's Navy Reserve obligation ended in 1956, he decided to enlist in the Air Force for training as an aviation cadet. He passed all the pretraining tests and was accepted into the program. Two years later, Gerald received his second lieutenant's bars, but his training wasn't over. He reported next to Helicopter Pilot's School at Randolph Air Force Base in Texas.

After completion of Helicopter Pilot's School, Lieutenant Young served at air bases in the Marshall Islands and Japan. Then he returned to the U.S. and was assigned to the Strategic Air Command until August 1967. During that time, he earned the rank of Captain.

Captain Young reported to the 37th Aerospace Rescue and Recovery Squadron at Da Nang, South Viet Nam in August 1967. A short time later, Captain Young's heroic acts during a rescue won him a Distinguished Flying Cross. He also received the Air Medal twice for his actions as a combat crew member. These awards are high honors, but Captain Young wasn't through with his heroic acts.

On November 8, 1967, word reached Da Nang Air Base that two rescue helicopters had been lost in an attempt to save a group of soldiers surrounded by enemy forces. The soldiers were in danger of being killed or captured, but their position in mountainous terrain and heavy enemy ground fire made a rescue almost impossible.

Finally, the call came down for volunteers to attempt another rescue after dark. Anxious to help the surrounded men, Captain Young polled his crew and found that they also were willing to volunteer. They immediately readied for the flight, learning that another rescue craft and several helicopter gunships would be making the trip.

On takeoff, it was decided that the other rescue helicopter would go in and pick up as many men as it could. Then Captain Young's helicopter would drop down and do the same.

The other helicopter landed and managed to

pick up three soldiers before heavy machine gun fire severely damaged the helicopter, forcing it to withdraw while still able.

By radio, the other helicopter's commander told Captain Young, "I got three soldiers, but the North Viets really tore up my ship. I'm heading back to Da Nang. You'd better come along. There are too many guns down there."

"I think we're going to chance it," Captain Young answered. "I'll see you at the base."

Then Captain Young called the supporting gun-ships. They informed him that they were low on fuel and ammunition, but they would stick around as long as they could.

Captain Young relayed all this information to his crew, and all of the men agreed to try for the rescue despite the dangers.

Then Captain Young and his copilot, Captain Ralph Brower of Stow, Ohio, hovered their heli-copter against the side of a slope and held that position. At the same time, the other members of the crew lifted soldiers into the helicopter.

When the last soldier was aboard, Captain Young moved his craft forward and upward, trying to avoid as much of the enemy fire as possible. The machine guns got to the helicopter, though, and it dropped to the ground, bursting into flames when it hit.

Flames leaped all over Captain Young's cloth-ing, but he still managed to kick open a window and escape from his ruined craft. Then he rolled on the ground, smothering the fire that had covered over 20 per cent of his body with second and third degree burns.

Despite the severe pain he felt, Captain Young got to his feet and began to search for survivors. He found an unconscious man who had been thrown from the helicopter and gave him first aid. After that, Captain Young started to look for other survivors, but he spotted enemy soldiers and hid from them.

The enemy soldiers began setting up their weapons to trap any further rescue helicopters. By this time, the pain in the American pilot's legs, an arm, and his body was terrifying, but he used his radio to warn other pilots. "They've set a trap," he said. "Forget about me. If I can get to a safe area, I'll signal you."

Then Captain Young crawled off to a new hiding place and examined his wounds. Realizing that the more serious burns needed bandaging, he covered them with the only materials he had — survival maps. After that, he heard enemy soldiers and knew that they were searching for him.

Captain Young went into shock from time to time, but he managed to keep out of the enemy's sight, walking and crawling about six miles. Finally, convinced that he had lost the enemy, he found an area clear enough for a helicopter landing and radioed for assistance. U.S. Air Force and Marine helicopters came to his rescue shortly after.

Back at Da Nang Air Base, Captain Young received treatment for his wounds. Then he was flown to the U.S. for additional treatment and skin grafts.

Six months later, Captain Young stood in the Inner Court of the Pentagon and listened, while President Johnson praised his extreme courage and awarded him the Medal of Honor.

After receiving his country's highest military award, Captain Young returned to active duty as a helicopter instructor pilot at Sheppard Air Force Base, Texas.